Tales U.R.B.A.N. Soldier

Volume 1

(Utterly Reckless Bullshit And Negativity)

Oh Gee

outskirts press

Tales of an U.R.B.A.N. Soldier
Volume 1
All Rights Reserved.
Copyright © 2020 Oh Gee
v2.0

This is a work of fiction. The events and characters described herein are imaginary and are not intended to refer to specific places or living persons. The opinions expressed in this manuscript are solely the opinions of the author and do not represent the opinions or thoughts of the publisher. The author has represented and warranted full ownership and/or legal right to publish all the materials in this book.

This book may not be reproduced, transmitted, or stored in whole or in part by any means, including graphic, electronic, or mechanical without the express written consent of the publisher except in the case of brief quotations embodied in critical articles and reviews.

Outskirts Press, Inc.
http://www.outskirtspress.com

Paperback ISBN: 978-1-9772-2399-9

Cover Photo © 2020 Omari Gill, Oh Gee. All rights reserved - used with permission.

Outskirts Press and the "OP" logo are trademarks belonging to Outskirts Press, Inc.

PRINTED IN THE UNITED STATES OF AMERICA

Contents

Tales of Other Poets

Black Angel	1
The Storm	9
Mind Games	10
The Night	12
Discovering my Inner self	13
The Unification of self	14

Tales of the People

Present Situation	19
Shutdown	20
Don't Sleep	22
P.S.A.	24
Rude Awakening	26
The System	27
Home of the Free Land of the Slaves	28
Our FUTURE	30
Nigga Please!	31
Sheep & Lions	33

Tales

ASSociates	39
The Five P's	41
Daydreaming	43
Time & Life	44
Declaration	46
Faith	48
Oblivious	49

Tales of the Heart

Trust Merry Go Round	53
Sugar to Shit	55
For the Duration	56

CHANGES	58
Single	61
GONE	62
Quest or Questions	64
Bad News	65
Sajata	67
Camelot	69
Obstacles	71

Tales of Oh Gee

Perception	75
My Perception	76
Individual ONE	77
Forward Thinking	79
True to Myself, Forever	80
Been here before	83
Contemplating	85
Growing Up	87
I'm Here	89
Journey	90
LIFE	92
Still Learning	95
Adversity	97
Confrontation	98
Coming or Going	100
Blessed	102
Boasting	104
RockStar	106
Mother's Model	107

Tales of the Hood

Botched Plan	111
Streets are watching	112
Any Day on the AVE.	114
Hell or Highwater	115

Tales of Other Poets

Black Angel	Bridgette Levi
The Storm	Donovan Zontarius Campbell
The Wave	Donovan Zontarius Campbell
Mind Games	Donovan Zontarius Campbell
Unification of Self	Dezarae Amira Gill
Finding My Inner Self	Dezarae Amira Gill

Black Angel

How dare she not think that she's pretty

Not think that she's beautiful

When asked how she rated her being

She,...

stated a seven

Giving her reflection

Dirty glances

Inquiries about skin enhancers

Thinking that lightening her skin

Would make her appear clean

Misconceiving

That only white angels get their wings

Shes....

gorgeous

And its more than just

her beautiful dark skin

Beautiful smile

and, her locs that she's had since before she was ten

she.....

has a quiet

"Old Soul" kinda disposition

and, at fourteen

She still watches

The Disney channel

Nickelodeon

And The animal planet

Four honors classes

If you have any questions

about your continent

or the earth and its axis

she'll answer it

she's,,.....

patient, kind, silly, sensitive

respectful,

at times moody

will take over your TV

but......

that's my baby.....

some years ago though

when she was about 6 or 7 years old

she surprised me

had me

secretly,

wiping the tears from my eyes

and, me

at that moment,

I had to be strong

so, patiently, i listened to what my baby had to tell me

she was sitting in my lap

and, as i'm braiding her hair into tiny little plats

she told me

she,...

wanted to be white

funny, when i was a little girl

i shared the same fight with my own identity

so the lauryn hill cd played

breaking the moments of quiet and monotony

i then, asked her why

she....

said she didnt like her hair nor her skin

but to her,

white peoples skin, hair, and eyes were pretty

I lifted my babies chin,

looked her in her beautiful brown eyes and grinned

....cant remember the words verbatim

but, for the sake of shaping this poem

this is pretty much how it went

"god made you who your are for a reason,

someone else's eyes, skin, and hair was not meant for you

but for god's choosins'

your beautiful black skin

happy to be natural and nappy hair

is what god gave you to wear

and, if you don't appreciate

then god may take it away

i try and teach her that true beauty cant be bought nor taught

keep your shoulders back

and your back straight

and your head held high

cuz see momma

wont be sending you to no head doctor

so they can lie

and, NOT tell you the truth

see they wont tell you

that you may be loos-ed

a few screws a time or two

may lose a few clues....

but, your self worth is not and ISSUE

IT'S YOUR TRUTH

you're not gonna be

depressed

repressed

havent been molested

wont always have the answers to lifes biggest tests

but anti-depressants will not be your BFF

i will not allow you to see your insecurities as an affliction

see, we're gona face them in that mirror

and give them the most beautifulist

adjectives (slash) descriptions

YOU ARE BLACK and that's a non-fiction(slash)fact

know that your dark skin does not make you the fallen one,

call up there to the "above" one

because you deserve all the rights

to that halo(slash)ring

and know that you are that beautiful black angel

for THE king

adorn the heavens with the choice to use your voice

keep singing

now, your signal has been sent

and for you,

those bells will keep ringing

my beautiful black one

my angel

tuck away your fears

wipe away your tears

cuz, god hears

and, sees all things

grab that mirror and look at your reflection of you

and you"ll see....

that blackgirls

black angels,

.....get there wings too

The Storm

As I sit here in this dark maze wondering what's next?

I only can begin to think of wrath of this world that is oh so cold through the face of death.

All of the ridicule, the scorn and even the abuse I still stand.

Not on the hands of world, but the hands of the man.

As He watches over me He begins to see, my struggle and then He begins to teach.

Teach a weary soul, one whom seems like a dark hole. Taketh in all of what the world has sold but has yet to hit gold.

This soul is weak, this soul is meek. This is divine, this soul is mine and I come to you weakened and battered.

But to those in which it matters know, I won't stay this way for long. Those who see, don't witness grief but witness a smile of the wounded.

As I give it all to Him, and know He's got it I just sit and wait.

Yet, still in this dark maze.

Mind Games

What are thoughts with no brain?

They can be vibrant, vivid perspectives without substance,

and as deep as Shakespearean romance.

What are thoughts that can't be conveyed to the depths of the world?

Failed ideas? Maybe, just maybe one wasn't brave enough to let the thought be heard.

Possibly the thought was so abstract that one became inferior to expressing.

One can be so consumed by the mind that a sense of self is lost.

Thoughts can consume one and turn them into an egregious character.

Thoughts cause heart aches and pain, as well as joy and laughter.

These same ideas are the walkway to a bevy of avenues that at different vantage points represent multiple scenarios of life.

It is found in those thoughts the souls that are engraved in the mind,

and one wonders, where might they be?

The lost ones usually kill the psyche, and paranoia breaches.

Wondering when, where and why is this person leaving?

Better yet was there a text? Is closure among us?

Chapter done book closed, now what's left?

One senses the end as the bottom is a long ways away.

The jump is made, but the thoughts and ideas remain.

why.........

The Night

Time's ticking

And she's dripping,

I think she knows.

As the look in her eyes pleads.

She lays anticipating penetration,

Her body in fire.

Desiring fornication, thinking,

That the attraction's predication dates back to just a few hours prior.

As he has his way, she moans and lays.

While she begs. "More, more. Harder, faster."

As this event comes to a close,

He reaches his peak and puts back on his clothes. Then leaves her.

Only for a night, she deceived her.

Discovering my Inner self

I've always had something to say

Then realized that it was called poetry

But I brushed it off because I knew I could be no floetry

Until my thoughts began to float from one subject to a verb

And it took no herb for me to realize I was high

High above the clouds

My thoughts became loud

I became frustrated with the headaches and heartaches until I felt I was about to break

Slowly stroking, taking the wind from me with every word written, I could hear speak that spoke and I knew in order to wake others I needed to be woke

Inhale the bullshit, exhale renewed, smoke

Clouding my vision, clearing through because I'm on a mission

Deeper than the incision of education, stronger than any dose of medication, what is my location?

What is getting all of my dedication?

I do it for you because if I help one after the other, word is bond and I want it to stick with you.

The Unification of self

Out of my body

Step into your body

Too often we've denied ourselves a yes because we've been told that we're NO.body

And I don't mean in a physical sense but more like unifying common sense

Without a fellow brethren I feel so tense because nothing makes sense!

Well maybe it's time for a cleanse

Lord forgive me for my sins

Looking through foggy lenses

Clouding my vision and affecting my decisions

Who am I? Who are we without unity?

Petty hurts when we could easily support the efforts and not disregard the step forward

Intertwined with a mental bond that I limit myself to.

Everyone else should be stuck with me right?

Imprisonment at its finest

My thoughts have mastered finesse but I feel naked because I'm stripped and involuntarily undressed with the facade continuously put on

I don't ask for a hand that will only land me face down stripped of my preordained crown

Crown royal on ice

Cold shoulders, stiff stares because try me if you dare

My mind is a natural disaster unless I focus on Him, my master but here in the physical, I ask for somebody to give enough of a damn that I don't end up in a dam where my voice is no longer heard

Then it becomes "I heard" because no one took the time to stop pretending to be nobody and unite so that you both could be somebody

So that it's no longer an out of body experience moreso a 20/20 experience because we've finally unified.

Deszarae Amira Gill

Tales of the People

Present Situation

Bombs going off in France

What's this world coming to, do we have a chance

Police killing Africans at an alarming rate

Is the end of the world coming, if so what'll be the date

Pedophiliacs pressing for lawful child molestation

What in the world, they're chipping away at the foundation

In what world does politicians care if SNAP recipients eat seafood or steak

Meanwhile Israel receives billions yearly from us, looks like they have a larger stake!

This world is crazy, this country is even more half- baked

Turning over our gold to these cronies was our worst mistake

Africans the only ethnicity in the world that doesn't practice unity

We have to get back to the commune, so we can get back to our communities

And in a perfect world, if there is such a thing

Just remember we'll be leaving this place to our offspring

Shutdown

Congress on the rag, doing shit outta spite

Effecting over a million Americans, it couldn't be right

Even though these guys are considered the opposite of extreme left

The things there're doing, could cause poverty, mayhem even death

They don't care and its more than evident

With them making over 3,000 a week, don't know about you but that's more than I've spent

People become united for matters of less standing

When it come to politicians, we should be more demanding

You see what they are doing, is nothing short of criminal

They are done sneaking, no more subliminal

So you can sit back relax and let it all happen

Or for fucking once, we can all finally come together

And do it as its meant, control the political weather

We the people control where the cash is

Without our backing, they couldn't be such asses

So people I challenge you, to shave your wool and grow your mane

You have my word, it'll never be the same

The second challenge is a bit more demanding, put aside prejudice and all our bias

And they won't be able to deny us!!!

Don't Sleep

Wake up, please arise from your slumber

Our people are being exterminated in record numbers

Most by our hands, the most is abortion

We must teach our youth, give them knowledge in the proper proportion

We are held to a different standard, but not by our own

We need to heighten our expectations, if not it won't be long

Before we are a non-factor, it won't matter that POTUS is black along with a ton of actors

It has been said we are the archetype, you know the first

Having that knowledge should make you want to burst

Instead it seems we're in a hurry to leave this world

Whether it's a block u don't own, or a girl

We continue to take life as if they belong to us

Nowadays when I see a group of youths don't know if I can trust

We have always been such a loving group

If you welcome negropeanism, your history becomes poop

We have no idea where we are going, cause we are ignorant to where we have been

Knowledge is the key, alpha and omega, beginning and end

It's one of few things that u can be greedy with and still share with the masses

Eat as much as you can, and u have my word, it won't produce gases

So this is my plea to my people

I challenge you to educate yourself and as many as you can

And we can thwart the powers that be master plan

To make this materialize, first and foremost, we have to beyond everything wake up

P.S.A.

African women, you're the mom of civilization

Turning up and twerkin, take a break from vacation

Let the weave go and all the European ways

I hope like hell, y'all grow out this phase

Nappy hair you consider it crappy

You've been convinced, if nappy not to be happy

Y'all complain when brothers fuck with the snowflakes

But y'all running around with blond wigs and blue contacts and that shit so fake

Y'all practice assimilation in the grandest fashion

When you see a brother with pink toes, you got the nerve to start bashing

Lashing out, disgusted with us

In order for our people to uprise, our queens are a must

I hope these word reach and make you feel some type of way

Hold on to yourself, I got plenty more to say

Don't worry ladies, we're guilty too

Calling sistahs bitches, no control over our britches

Making children and bouncing out the back

I feel you ladies, that shit is super whack

Africans worldwide, we're in a state of emergency

We need to do something about it, with a sense of urgency

Times running out, the sands almost gone

Unify immediately, right all our wrongs

America and whole world, will be singing a different song

I hope you take this message raw, with no salt

If we don't take action, it will be all of our fault!!

Rude Awakening

Why should I respect the laws, they don't respect us

Pigs shooting unarmed kids, as if it's just

Something has to change and I mean quick

Or else these pigs can get roasted on a spit

It's a couple of things about America I just don't get

This land was built off genocide, rape and things of the like

So when we mirror what we were taught, white supremacy shows it's might

The pharmaceutical industry sells drugs all year long

So when I come up with a mixture in the kitchen and hit the corner, how am I wrong

This country is a mess, to say the least

What they don't realize, is that these conditions create proverbial beast

That's it America you've had it how you wanted

The spirit of a million slaves, that's right this bitch is haunted

We're fed up, the bullshit has reached it's limit

We are no longer falling for cheap tricks and gimmicks

We're playing for keeps, no losses to be had

So I call out to all my friends, associates and comrades

The System

Minimum wage creates maximum rage

This is with what we are faced, in this day and age

Everything rises, except for morality and pay

With low pay and scruples, these might be the last days

On meager earnings, they expect you to make it

If you can't afford it, they lock you up when you take it

So you rob Paul to pay Peter

Electricity and water up for disconnect, which one can you do without?, neither

So do you take a bath in the dark?

Or do you inhale the filth, in the light?

Which ever one you choose, mentally you won't be right

Settle for minimum wage or go for the maximum gamble

No matter what, you're caught in a never ending scramble

The way this game is set, you're meant to be a slave

So in that case, I'll create my own path

Whether it's a dirt road or its paved!!

Home of the Free Land of the Slaves

America is the greatest country and that's no lie

Their the greatest at stealing, lying and having lame alibis

They start wars for selfish reasons

Usually money motivated, sounds like treason

Land of the free and home of the brave

Free to steal what they want, including humans as slaves

Oil from the Middle East, gold from the motherland

Gotta stop conforming, come up with another plan

Take this country back, divide it among the people

Stop giving your money to every mosque, temple or steeple

Religion another faction to keep us divided

There's only one race and that's human and we all provide it

With out the poor to do the riches bidding

We run this, not them, are you fucking kidding

Conform to the system and you will come up short

The problem starts, when we go to them, instead of creating our own support

And to the republic, for which it stands

From the way look of things, we're not in the plans

So continue to believe what you hear

Or form your own conclusion, look at what's happening around here

What can we do, uprise fast, couldn't be more clear

What we can't do, is give in or indulge in fear

Our FUTURE

People today often complain about the behavior of our youth

I'll share with you, the pure unadulterated truth

When it comes to their behavior, the blame has been sorely misplaced

If your familiar with tv, the web or music today

Part of the answer is staring you smack dab in the face

The other reason for this condition is not so public and it's kind of crummy

Parents these days are raising fake gangsters, label whores and dummies

I've witnessed mothers on Facebook, while their children run amuck

But when you make mention to this, then they have words to lend, to you, no less and I'm like what the fuck !

Discipline has been stripped from the home, like a football from a running backs grip

The family structure in America is sinking, like that titanic ship

What ever happened to it takes a village to raise a child

Somewhere along the line we've forgotten, as a result our youth runs utterly wild

So before you blame the kids take a deeper look into the matter

So next time you witness a rowdy youth carrying on, just know it might be the latter

Nigga Please!

Stop killing our army, we're at war

Make no mistake, these people have much more in store

We execute our people for this and that

We are losing momentum, increasing fucked up stats

Modern day genocide, being performed by blacks

All in the name of lunacy and chasing stacks

Telling you to wake up, has become quite cliche

With our sheepish behavior I don't know what else to say

I'm at a loss for words but I'm ready for action

As time goes on we are losing plenty of traction

That's right we are doing the opposite of what it takes to win

If we keep pussy footing around, this will be the end

We were the first to civilize the earth

Somewhere along the way, we've forgotten our worth

Don't you worry, I'm here to remind you

I dont do subliminal, or dropping clues

I bring it direct, smack dab in your grill

Giving you a message you can comprehend and feel

I implore you to take a positive stand

Stop fucking killing each other, you might as well be the klu klux klan!!

Sheep & Lions

Leave the herd, join the pack

Cause being slaughtered, is not where it's at

Not slaughtered in a literal sense

As fucked up as it is, you think it's just coincidence?

Expand your iris, remove your heads from the sand

No bullshit people, we need a plan

Make no mistake, we need one of action

Protest and marching, doesn't provide enough satisfaction

Don't misunderstand, violence is the last rung on the ladder

If "We The People" keep fucking around it won't matter

It's time to hold politics accountable for its actions

Maybe replace them with another faction

Besides the issues r not political, it's one of social agenda

Ponder on how this country was constructed, sit back and remember

Swindled geography, stolen legacies and enslaved humans

No wonder the U S in almost in ruins

GMO's in our food, without our permission

How in the hell did we make it into this condition

Kids not really confident about their gender, nor do they respect parents

Less school, discipline stripped, are a couple of things responsible for these events

Jobs are gone, shipped overseas

That wouldn't happen, if they cared about our needs

Leave the herd and join the pack

Become a lion and let's get them off our back

If we continue our sheepish ways

They're right these are the last days

It's been said that the meek shall inherit the earth

If we follow their prophecy, when we get it, what will it be worth?

Tales

The City of Wind

Let me start out by dropping facts

Once I do, you'll know why we act the way we act

People think our nickname is because of the weather

No, it's cause in the 1920's, at world fairs there was no one better

So we bragged and boasted about our town

And then proved it was the best around

So when they call my city windy

It's not that its any more than Indy

We talk plenty shit and we can back up the smell

Anyone whose actually been in the city knows this quite well

There are many layers to my city

Can't think of one that contains pity

The first I would say is the hustle

Without this, you're missing you're true chi-town muscle

The next would be the city's dynamics

Racially divided, highly violent, those parts I can't stand it

The food is world renowned

Shit! Harold's chicken and Eli's cheesecake came from my

town

Haven't lived there for years but its the place I call home

When I visit, I still know where to and where not to roam

Similar to Caesar, if he was to revisit Rome

If I was to die and come back I would still consider it home

My city has taught me countless, valuable lessons

I guess that's why, when adversities arise, I don't indulge in stressing

It's best to be a quick study and not a slow comprehender

Our senses are keen, we sniff out pretenders

Mind your business you might be fine

Encounter the wrong apple, you've already crossed the line

Don't strap your boots on, will be viewed as a broke joke

Once they see you coming, trying their best to provoke

Nerves of steel and a sense about yourself

Don't have either of those, stay in the house, you know on the shelf

It's definitely a city of show and prove

Gotta know how to talk and how to move

Well I can't tell it all, that would be lame

Go live it like I did, I swear, you'll never be the same!!

ASSociates

All my friends seem to think about is sex

I often wonder if they care what's next

Their actions reflect that they are living for the day

They've got to know there's a better way

Useless days and fruitless nights

Subconsciously have they given up the good fight?

I hope not, cause I'll be forced to go right

Out the door, cause outta my life I need more

No time for BS, my schedule full, if that's not what your on, there's the door

Got my eye on the big picture, no minuscule items

If your not on what I'm on, can't be tight with'em

They say if you wanna be successful, surround yourself with folks of the like

Haven't given it a gang of thought but then again I just might

Reinvent myself for the better

Prepare myself for any weather

Whether that means shaking a few so- called friends

So I can get more acquainted with my ends

Or staying to my own

With this new approach would I be wrong?

At any rate, make no mistake success is mine for the take

The changes I make, are gonna be welcome

The time I have for fake, quite seldom

When the word friend enters my mind

I don't know what to think

Then I slowly recall, certain instances, the answer starts to sink

Into my brain, I start to travel

The word friendship, starts to unravel

Like a spool of yarn, knots in bunches

Until you fix this limited function

Similar to friendship and the bullshit that arises

You can fix the mess of move on to new horizons

The sun looks great if into the distance

To arrive, must pay with a bit of persistence

Those crab in a barrel are getting stronger by the day

Gotta do what I can, to stay away

One true friend I know I have indeed

That friend is me and that's all I need!!

The Five P's

Living life properly prepared

Can help prevent poor performance

Perform correctly you can live life enormous

As far as the size that's up to the individual

Slight warning living this way can make you quite critical

Preparation provides more time to think

So when you approach a situation u can create the best link

You can apply this principle to just about any aspect of life

It can be the difference in doing a project with a flathead or a butter knife

Also pertains to monetary gains

Spending, for the big picture, sometimes you have to refrain

Being poor in any sense, is not fortune by any means

So in this case, why would you want your performance to be?

This just a tale of order, confidence and time

Everybody goes thru their form of chaos

But getting a jump on things, could be the difference between a dollar and a dime running in & out of time

But getting the jump on things, could be the difference between laughing and crying. Living and dying. Loving or lying. Staying or leaving. Rejoicing or grieving. Keeping your liquor down or heaving. Homework done in the afternoon or evening. Having money in your account or borrowing to next weekend.

Daydreaming

As the sun shines and the wind blows

Where will this day take me?, I don't know

Positive as ever, head held high

The universe is vast, just look at the sky

Clouds on the move, birds flying in flocks

Sitting by the river, watching fish, skipping rocks

Enjoying the universe, and all it has to give

Take advantage of your life and make sure you live

My veins are as deep as rivers

Everytime I wake, they deliver

The universe is my ally

It will be till I die

Only in a physical sense

Cause my soul is eternal, I've known this every since

I took my trip through the womb

I'm here for great reasons I presume

Words flow freely, from the pen to the paper

When you think about it, it's the ultimate caper

So I'll put my thoughts, life and opinion in print

And above all, without a doubt, I will represent

Time & Life

Everyday new opportunities await

Attitude &actions determine your fate

Perception &intelligence influence your ability to relate

A few ingredients to success contained above

U can try it with no rules or show yourself some love

Life is full of mountains &valleys

You decide if you want to drink from fountains or live in alleys

Take a bite out of life, don't be afraid to chew

So when adversities rear their head, you'll know what to do

Life is what you make it, you're the only chef

Only you determine what's what, from your 1st step to your last breath

Opportunities seized, opportunities lost

The effort u wanna pay you set the cost

Whether u build your own empire, or the next person is your boss

Dreams are dreams, unless you put forth action

Done correctly, effort &results closely matching

Time is life & life is time

So when it comes to my life don't waste mine

I live my time the way I desire

I refuse to waste my life being a cryer

Once you lose time, you won't find it again

So when it comes to life, I'm gonna win

Our life is short, can't take it for granted

Once you spend your time, you can't recant it

Life is good, life is grand

Plan your work and work your plan

Use time wisely, take full advantage

1440 minutes in a day you can manage

You can make excuses or you can make a way

Be the author of your own story, narrator of your play

From the time you're conceived

To the time you're achieved

From the cradle to the casket

Live life, don't neglect to bask in it

Time and life two synonymous terms

The more time you live, the more life you confirm

Declaration

As dawn cracks and the alarm sounds

Once again it's time to put it down

Handling this, doing that

I'm a dawg, I don't fuck with you cats

Staying to myself, focused on the mission at hand

Sticking to the script, not straying from the plan

Accomplishing my goals, becoming the man

I'm focused so hard, my head is starting to spin

I'm seeing results, I'll see this thru till the end

Once my project drops, will it flop

Will it do massive numbers or fall flat like lumber chopped

At any rate, going to put it out regardless

Show y'all my skills as an artist

Some will love it and some won't

Not really worried about the ones that don't

With my work, I hope to inspire plenty

Hell I'll be satisfied to inspire any

Last but not least, can't wait till I'm finish

I hope that censors, do not diminish

The message I'm looking to convey

Just wait, I have plenty to say

Faith

Things seem to happen for one reason or another

If you're not careful, situations can overwhelm & smother

If you operate off faith, you know, a sense in knowing

Things have a way of working itself out, as long as you keep going

Staying positive is essential

Practicing this, maximizes your potential

Hope for the best, stay prepared for the worst

Above all, remember to keep yourself first

May sound selfish, I feel your thoughts

But if you can't do for yourself, can't worry about others and what hasn't been bought

So keep a stiff upper lip, head held high

Sometimes a positive attitude is enough to get by

Trust me when I tell you, this works like a charm

Keep calm, cool and collective, no need for alarm

I've been living this way, for quite sometime

That's how I'm able to convey it to you, in the form of verses and rhymes

Oblivious

Look at ole girl

She lives in a small little world

One where everything she does is excusable

Character, set by unseen actions, once done, irremovable

She swear she's the sun, cause around her everything revolves

Problems arise, she doesn't lend her self to solve

She will lend fingers, only to point

Petty contribution, what's the fucking point

Yeah she's hopeless, scarred as they come

If you knew her story, you might not consider her young, dumb and full of cum

Everyone has a saga, a story if you will

They display truth, lies, crimes, alibis, reasons good and bad, that's only one thrill !

Lady be mindful of your surroundings

Before u no it, in a pine box underground , is what you'll be found in

Don't be so caught up in your own dealings

That you're oblivious to others feelings

So when you think your baseless peruse, is not somebody being used or abused

You got another thing coming, it's called karma, shake her hand

I see it in your eyes, spaghetti legs, you can barely stand!

Tales of the Heart

Trust Merry Go Round

Trust is a must, in my dealings

Especially when I decide to expose my feelings

I'm sensitive by nature, rough in appearance

When bullshit rears its head, I run interference

Before my heart gets involved, my brain has to give clearance

I know I'm not perfect, still I refuse to settle

But still I go on with exemplary mettle

Crossing my T's and dotting my I's

Getting myself together, so I can fly high

Once I meet her, bring her up to the atmosphere

Fly all day, holding her close, keeping her near

Before I invite her on this grand journey

I must make sure that she's not here to burn me

I've been singed before and it's not beneficial

I refuse to let my feelings be used as sacrificial

So I choose to leave my feelings, locked in a vault

I guess I was made that way, by default

Until the right women comes along, with the key and combination

The key to it being the right one, is the correct combination

Beauty from within, with honesty pouring out

I've encountered beautiful women but usually the truth, they come without

Back on my journey, living my time to the fullest

Fully aware, taking my time, dodging relationship bullets

I don't have an issue with relationships as a whole

My issue is when the ship sinks and you end up in an emotional hole

I know she's out there, the one I want and need

Can't wait until I find her, so my heart can stop this constant bleed!!

Sugar to Shit

U can't change me,so stop trying

Your emotions don't phase me, so stop crying

I'm not the best,but the best you've had

Sounds like u got issues go take it up with your dad !

I'm saying that, to say this, under pressure I don't bend,break or fold

You know what you've been told and what you've been showed!

So it's time to show and prove

Take heed to these words because you I don't want to lose

With that being said take this how you want no need for translation

Just stopped by to drop a little information

In closing I will leave you with this

Bullshit and games I've never tolerated and I speak my mind 99.9% of the time and if you can't deal with that I don't know what to tell you

If something doesn't give there will be no more us BOO!!

For the Duration

Dear Angeletta, words can't express

How dear you are to me and how I've been blessed

An individual that can match me on every front

I've paid my dues, I finally got who I want

You're one hell of a women, to say the least

The love you provide, can't wait to see the justice of the peace

You wear many hats and still have room to grow

Since our first kiss, I haven't been on the other side of your door

With you, the globe, I would love to explore

Je- Taun you're my umbrella in the pouring rain

Loving you is easy, there's no strain

I know the feeling is mutual, for this I am sure

When I'm in your arms, I couldn't feel more secure

Mrs. Williams, only for the time being

Once you take my last name, it couldn't be more freeing

Us together as one, through the thin and the thick

Bonnie and Clyde for the rest of the flick

So how bout it baby, let's take over the planet

And not give a fuck, if the haters can stand it

To Be Continued.............

CHANGES

The feeling I'm feeling is a mile past frustrated

I've never felt so down trodden and mentally castrated

I hang in there for the sake of not quitting

Somewhere along the way, I've seemed to have forgot, it's myself that I'm bullshitting

For the sake of staying sane I have to make an alteration

Whether it's my habits, my approach or my location

At any rate a change is more than welcome

Who knows when I was here, whether or not they felt him

I'm not satisfied in this space

What do I change or replace

Will it be my attitude, surroundings or my position

It might just be a trifecta, to improve my condition

Once the pressure builds, will the levy break

Has all of this been a waste of time, one giant mistake

All the hot, steamy nights and the well intentions

In order for the levy to hold, I guess we'll need some sort of intervention

The closer I get to you, the colder I get

If we continue, will I be filled with discontent and regret

I've conveyed to you before

If this doesn't work, there will be no more

No more hugs, no more kisses

All I will have for someone, are frequent misses

Relationships, I've had my fill

I refuse to be part of another raw deal

Solo, I'll be lonely, for this I have no doubt

On the other hand, I'll be done trying to figure this bullshit out

I've reached my limit, giving of myself only to get nothing in return

My brain is fucking fed up, when will this stupid heart of mine learn?

Adventures in life, they come and they go

These relationship escapades, they really blow!

Just for once, can I find one who's honest?

Not so willing to recant their words, so quick to break a promise

This game called life, has unlimited ups and downs

You can celebrate the smiles or you can ponder on the frowns

What I refuse to do is, continually be let down

Thinking the best of people, giving the benefit of the doubt

I don't want to be evil but I need another route

As tough as it is to keep your feelings on an even keel

I'm as genuine as they come, so I don't know anything but keeping it real

So I strive forward, knowing perfection is unattainable

I continue pushing on, looking for a love that's sustainable

For once can I find one who will give as much effort as me

As far as that goes, I have yet to see

Single

Being alone is sometimes what I prefer

Expressing my feelings to others, I'd rather defer

Until I find that one who is worth the risk

I guess I'll continue to carry on like this

Will I find her or will she seek me out

At any rate I'll be happy, for this I have know doubt

Your relationship status, please don't let it define you

Instead take plenty of time out to find you

I've spent a few decades on this earth

I've spent most of it determining my worth

Don't be confused, I'm not after a lady that's perfect

I desire one soul, who knows how to work it

The ying to my yang, the fuse to my bang

The sweat on my brow, the "O" in my wow

Able to finish my sentence, able to help me avoid repentance

Perhaps at the right time, we will cross paths

Or maybe I already have, in that case, no need to calculate the math

I'll stand alone for the duration of my Infiniti

If that's the case, no holy matrimony, no one else to be kin to me!

GONE

Her beauty is a heated pool, ready for me to dive

Until I met her didn't know what it felt like to be alive

Her actions are sweet words even sweeter

I thank the universe, that I had my time, to meet her

Her eyes had a sparkle, her body had a twist

Conversation off the hook, couldn't wait to kiss

Had that first kiss couldn't explain it

Can't wait for a man of the cloth to ordain it

Neglected to mention the intelligence factor

Personality pleasant, never sensed she was an actor

The way I feel, don't want to, nor do I fear it

If she was a sample, couldn't wait for her to clear it

She's the baseline to my song

The right to my wrong

The bop in my stride

As my queen by my side

Riding shotgun for the long ride

Off into the sunset or sky filled with clouds

Shining off each other, standouts in any crowd

Lady of the hour, too sweet to be sour

U&I as one, everlasting love power

Quest or Questions

Will I be single for the duration?

Never know the feel of a family vacation

Continue in various acts of fornication

Hopefully I'll experience matrimonial elation

Till death does us part, sounds about right

Someone I can hold, other than just at night

I can be galant, gentlemen of gentlemen, a shining armored knight

Once I get hitched, I won't give up, even with a fight

It's been close to forty years and I've never proposed

I guess I haven't found what I'm looking for I suppose

Looking for someone I can share with, accomplish similar goals

Someone I can spend countless time with, dining out and evening shows

I won't settle, not even in a pinch

No ugly personality, can't deal with a grinch

Size isn't important but the size of her heart is

The way she prepares a meal and handle her biz

I write these words as a friendly reminder

Won't know who I want until I find her

Bad News

Listened to my voicemail , just received the heart- wrenching news

Needless to say, once I listened, wanted to cry the blues

Believe it or not, I'm happy for you

But for myself, don't know what to do

Well we said it in the beginning, if its meant to be it will

I'm still here as your friend, yet in still

I don't suspect my feelings for you will change

If there is a next time, maybe we will be closer in range

Here I go, back to square one

Back on my life long quest for the one

One thing I dunno, with time I'll be just fine

Another thing, never will let you off my mind

Lastly I wish you and dude the best

This time hopefully he'll be better than the rest

No one can take away our times we shared

The conversations we had, the truths we bared

Lets not forget the chicken wing dinner

Oh yeah good times, now that was a winner

A trip to the grocery store, on your dime

Sajata I just want to let you know, I did and still do appreciate your time!!

Sajata

I love your versatility

The distance between us is hurting my feelings

Not the miles but the level of our dealings

I've told you before how I feel

I'm ready to find some of you to steal

I miss u and your body and your spirit

I need you to really listen to really hear it

I want u as my queen and nothing less

'Cause compared to what I've met you are the best

Your a beautiful person inside and out

I want u on another level, for this I have no doubt

From a spark, to a major fire

Me without you, no truth, I'm a liar

Your smile is electrifying

Don't know what else I should be trying

You've seen it all, lows and the highs

And you still continue to gaze upon me with those gorgeous eyes

Your heart is what I'm after

Don't get me wrong, I enjoy the convo and laughter

Just your friendship, I'm not willing to settle

Give it a while you'll admire my mettle

That's all for now I'll leave you to think

And I know u feel me and you're on the brink

Cause I've hit you with everything but the kitchen sink !

Camelot

I'm your knight in shining armor

Something like a charmer

Excited or upset I know how to calm ya

I'm the man of your dreams

Plenty of self- esteem

Swag by the pound

I keep ya without a frown

Enough about me, what's up with you?

Tell me your hobbies, what you like to do

Walks in the park, trips to the zoo?

Shopping or fine dining, we can do that too

First let me tell ya, don't play no games

Just as quick as I met ya, I can forget yo name

No ordinary women, hope you feel my pain

I've been tricked & treated by the best of them

Trust me girl not like the rest of hims

So take the time out and invest in him

    (hook)

Yeah that's it, yeah girl you got it

Don't front girl, you like what you spotted

I'm the T.N. stands for that nigga

Don't sell drugs or pull triggers

Trust me girl I'm an extraordinary figure

Second part of the story

Same category

I'm the man of the hour

Too sweet to be sour

Give yourself a chance, I got the power

Tall dark & attractive

Far from hyperactive

Cool, calm & dapper

Far from your average rapper

This is what u should be after

I know I'm bragadocious

Spitting quite ferocious

I'm the host with the most

Kicking it on each and every coast

Chi- town born & bread

Come on girl, don't front with that head

U heard what I said!!!!

Obstacles

I'm sitting here going thru it

Really don't know what to do with

Myself general or specific

Gotta make a change, so life can be terrific

I'm steadfast in my decisions, gotta make better ones

No more head on collisions, with my self that is

Gotta stop bullshitting and handle my biz

I think I'll try on kid gloves, stop being so aggressive

With this new approach, I'll be more impressive

Have to use my third eye instead the two

That way I know, I'll get my just due

I've had obstacles before, never this great

If I fall victim to negativity, won't be able to open the gate

Keep my attitude pure, my thoughts even better

Me and success will finally be together

This is easier said than done, focus must be kept

Gotta keep my blinders on and watch every step

Carefully planned, ruthless execution

True to myself, no prostitution

Belief in my self is essential

Time to make it happen, fuck potential

My injury has changed my life forever

From here on out, I will conquer each and every endeavor

Tales of Oh Gee

Perception

They say think outside the box, I never knew one existed

That's why I don't conform, they must have got me twisted

I'm an individual, in every facet of the word

Not being who you are, is quite absurd

So I strive to be the best me that I can accomplish

I refuse, to swim with the ordinary fish

I'm a man before anything, this I know for sure

Living this mediocre existence, how much more can I endure

I stay faithful and practice humility

I keep my stiff arm out, so no one cane get to me

Focused on my plan, planned on my focus

Nothing can stop me, not even a hoard of locusts

Using every opportunity to avoid obstacles and every obstacle as an opportunity

Living life in these conditions is nothing new to me

So I step cautiously and faithfully all in the same stride

Keep my dreams and reality on the same track, so they collide

My visions are clear, my path not so crystal

So I keep my thoughts pure, eyes peeled and hand on my pistol

My Perception

I've been scolded as long as the life I've lived

I've tried my best to be me, wasn't good enough to give

In that case I'll stay to myself, with that I am fine

Can't go through life without being genuine

If they can't accept me that's their trouble

Can't spend the rest of my life worrying about their bubble

I've been scolded for as long as I can recall

The same ones that scold, do nothing to help when you fall

So unless your criticism is constructive keep your syllables to yourself

Your opinion about me, is smaller than an elf

If you don't like me, that's your fucking issue

You crying,'bout that?, what about, when the kids need a tissue

The problem is, your focused in the wrong direction

Put that energy into yourself, fix your own imperfections

People gone talk about u, hell I do it too

But I stay away from scolding, not my feelings, so what gives me the right to?

Individual ONE

I don't struggle to blend in, I strive to standout

I might do something twice but never the same route

It's better to be deep in thought, than shallow in misery

The way some act, they seem to be kids to me

Juvenile actions, expecting adult results

With this as your plight, my intelligence this insults

With every second that passes, I strive to grow

From the person I was seconds ago, unknown facts I want to know

Conformity has never been an option, because I'm a true individual

Living my life in this fashion, has definitely created residuals

I embrace them all, whether great or unfavorable

Simply because these things are what able me

To claim the status of a true separate being

Living this way, has been the most freeing

Independence in abundance, responsibility necessary

If not, a gang of jail time, this could carry

Don't say it if you can't display it

You got one life and it's nothing to play with

Everything else you have to learn on your own

How in the hell do you think I got so grown!

Forward Thinking

Goals set, six years till I retire

With my work, many people I hope to inspire

Mid forties not society's ideal age, to get out of the rat race

Fortunately, I'm intelligent enough to set my own pace

Haven't ever been a fan of conformity or the actions of the masses

Take a look at what's going on or perhaps you need glasses

People working all their being, until they reach the grave

Wake up, take your head out of the sand, you're nothing but a slave

I refuse to be a house or a field nigger

As a matter of fact, I've been groomed to be something bigger

Author of my own destiny, so to speak

Stay tuned, watch and learn, as I reach my peak

I'm a lot of things and its a lot I've never been

Doing it my way, not theirs, I'm destined to win

It's your choice, take a stand, devise your own route

Or stay in the maze, get your cheese, which holds no clout

With those views being conveyed

Make your decision, the BS they spew, I've never obeyed!

True to Myself, Forever

Best kept secret, didn't even know it

Couldn't guess on they best day,

I was Put hear to flow it

Poet, term reserved for tight writers

iPhone used, no tendinitis

Vocab been anti status quo

Blame mama, also Chicago

Constantly press to be the best

No matter the task or the test

Been writing since a second grader

Word problems first love on paper

Next episode think it was the 5th

By then just knew I had the gift

This time girls were my angle

Very first time I let my heart dangle

Tell u one thing, boy did I regret

I know one thing, never did forget

Forgot about poetry, feelings hurt

Got to pick my self from the dirt

Next year Rakim and Too Short appearance

Couldn't believe what I was hearing

Passion reignited, I was still fearing

Kept it to myself this round

But I let her keep me down

Now I'm grown, not in Omari's town

Could give a shit less how u feel

Could've had books published, bitch r u 4 real??!!!!

Now u know y my attitude is such

Y y'all think I don't give 2 fucks

Flow was fluid from the start

But I let this chick change my part

In my own life, ain't that a bitch

Flows still stanky imma be the shit

The point of this tale is simple as it gets

Gotta live your life with minimal regrets

Never let the next person cash in yo bets

Firm believer every action happens for a reason

Take consideration into who u choose pleasin'

If u give a fuck, what do give yourself

Let no one make U put U on the shelf!!!

That last point can't stress that enough

Get it sooner than I did life will be less rough!

Get ready , I made my decision

That's it, I'm coming for my division

Chop, slice, part whatever u call it

Fulfilling my dream and filling my wallet

Best kept secret, it's out the bag

Who would've ever known what a gift I had!!!!!!

    P.S. True Story!

Been here before

So..... Looks like I'm back in this rat race, I'm not even a mouse

Gotta put myself back in competition, to pay for my house

My money coming slow, so I gotta do what a man can

To keep me from having the lower hand

Life cold but it's fair

Dependent upon your decisions, it can be a nightmare

It's me that controls my dream

I've been my own worst enemy or so it seems

Time to follow another's program, until I create my own

I will finally be able to take my rightful place, on the throne

To be the king, that I was intended

All this knowledge that I've acquired, lets hope I didn't spend it

Early to bed, early to rise

Life always brings a surprise

Get it while you can, stick to the plan

Get it under wraps, like yo name was Saran

It's up to you, nobody else

Make sure you play for keeps or get left on the shelf

Life is short, go for the glory

Take time out, to make your own story

Audacious as ever, a level past clever

I keep it unafraid , on every endeavor

I know my times running, so I'm clocking in

I know you hear the music, maybe the violin

Or perhaps it's the piano, keys play a sweet tune

My time is surely coming, from sunrise to the moon

Contemplating

I feel like life has passed me by

I don't remember when but I do know why

Rash decisions even worst reactions

Maybe I want too much, overall satisfaction

Maybe I set my bar too high

Lately all I can do is sigh

About missed chances and self inflicted circumstances

I am who I am, can't assume anyone else's identity

I assume I'll continue my quest for serenity

I've come too far to turn back now

Press on with the when, why and the how

Life is filled with peaks and valleys, lows and highs

Plenty of helloes, as well as goodbyes

I love it all, the pain and the pleasure

For what I've been through, no one could measure

My attitude, the reason I do things as I see fit

Why I take everything with so much grit

It's the reason I love with so much passion

It's frightened ordinary women, when I display it in that fashion

Who am I kidding, I still have years yet to live

I still have much of myself yet to give

My heart and burden kinda heavy these days

Should I continue as I've been or change my ways

I'm sick and tired of heartbreak and dismay

Without taking chances and throwing caution to the wind

How will I make my means to an end

Without that special someone, how will I live happily ever after

Will I go through unnecessary pain, forever evading eternal laughter?

Growing Up

A lot of vice lord mixed with a gang of gangster

The city of Chicago I'd really like to thank ya

The streets were an education

But school was my fun

Never carried a knife

But I still tote a gun

I am what I am, it is what it is

The streets of the Chi taught me to handle my biz

Doing things that grown people did, as a kid

The Windy City made me grow up swift

Drinking alcohol, smoking on spliffs

Barely a teen, getting plenty sex

At the age of 14, you couldn't imagine what was next

Gang banging, selling coke

The streets of my city, no fucking joke

Went and got tats on my own

Knowing my mom would not condone

Didn't really care thought I knew it all

When I got in trouble, she was the first I would call

The lessons she would preach, I didn't wanna listen

Now that I'm an adult, I give the same to my kids, only my rendition

My city taught me a lot, I'm thankful for that

If it wasn't for my mama and my city don't know where I would be at

I'm Here

As I lie here with thousands a thought

One resonates as the juggernaut

Once I start back walking, will it be a hobble

Or will my foot or ankle give out and wobble

At any rate, I'm ready for whatever

You see, I was created a level past clever

I could take the easy way out, collect disability, sit back and smile

While my life waste away all the while

Failure is not a discussion, especially in this case

I couldn't gaze squarely in the mirror at that face

I'm one if the universe's most resilient souls

I reject the idea of not accomplishing my goals

I'm stubborn that way, guess I'm an ass

Who cares you and I, we work from a different hourglass

With God and I on my side, no one can arrest my stride

With that as my strategy, there's no where success can hide

With that being said I know I can make it

Big question is can the world take it?

Journey

Here I sit pissed as ever

Back to work, on my next endeavor

Sit down work, could be worse

Gotta milk it out, put me first

Can't wait until this process is done

No workers comp, no physical therapy

When I walk people won't stare at me

Ok I get it, I'm now what they consider disabled

As long as there's will in my power, that a fable

They say every thing happens for one reason or the other

When this shit happened, all I could think of was my mother

She taught me its not what happens but how it's handled

Can't lie y'all felt like I've been the victim of a vandal

My whole being shook, to legs of spaghetti

With what I sustained, will I be ready?

To get back out there live life to the fullest

Or give up, resort to the streets, take a chance on being riddled with bullets

What ever happens, I'm ready for the results

Basking in the glory of success or sustaining ridicule and various insults

When all the smoke clears I'll still be me

If I'm sailing the oceans or drowning in the sea !

LIFE

Trials and tribulations, seem to follow me in bunches

I'm seem to get myself into the damnedest crunches

No car, no money damn this blows

Sometimes in life, it's just the way it goes

So I take deep breath and continue to plow

Cause giving up and feeling sorry, I just don't know how

They say when life gives you lemons, you should make lemonade

I'd rather be the grand marshal in my own parade

One thing I know, gonna make myself a promise

Gonna keep my word to myself, honest

I've also come to this conclusion

Make better decisions, have less life contusions

All of this sounds good, as long as I follow thru

The same instances happen, by now I should know what to do

Life can be humorous at times

Lateral moves, vertical climbs

Challenging situations, fun times in bunches

Time moves on, so we are constantly under deadline crunches

Unexpected situations, met with rash decisions and certain malice

Beating on my chest and swinging my phallus

I need the humility of a shoeshiner, instead attitude of a peacock

I brag from the top of my head, to my soles, stepping on rocks

If I don't put me on a pedestal, who can I trust to this task?

No one, so I continue on my journey, seeking out success, in which to bask

My focus is stern, my actions more rigid

Won't give up, press on writing, until y'all get it

I'm here for the duration, might as well make it the best

Here you can witness, my deepest most intimate thoughts, undressed

You get a tour of my train of thought

Adversities I've faced, battles that are still fought

Victories are present, not as abundant as the losses

I've had plenty of women as well as bosses

One thing has been constant, throughout the whole flick

That constant is I , from the different gigs and chicks

I have so much life left to get, more victories to be obtained

I move with a purpose now, from stupid shit I choose to refrain

Still Learning

The odds are against me, this is nothing new for the kid

Brushing off tough times, continually submitting my bid

No ears for the naysayers, no time for negative conversation

Hell I have an appointment to keep, with the entire nation

I've always felt like a professor or something of the sort

I'm the starting point guard, the ball is in my court

Bringing you line after line of certain situations, from my life and times

Obstacles in my path, gotta use a preposition

Put my blinders on, intended to change my position

How ever it goes, accepting yes's or dealing with no's

Doing live shows or putting down flows

To the grindstone, I plan to keep my nose

Life can be difficult, for this I have no doubt

I'm 38 years young, still attempting to figure out

My purpose and what life is all about

The more I write, the closer I seem to get

Mistakes I've made in the past, never want to forget

They say if you don't know your history, you'll be doomed

to repeat it

Trials, tribulations and pain I've experienced, never want to delete it

You see what I've been through, is what makes Omari me

All I can achieve is to be the best Omari I can be

I've done dumb things in the past, I still have less than intelligent moments

The thing about me is, no matter what, I'll stand tall as a man and own it!!

Adversity

Foot sitting here, throbbing like a lung

Stairs quite difficult don't know about a ladder rung

My foot screwed up bad, now it's feeling worse

Every time I take step at work wanna yell out and curse

Pain is the reason for this verse

I've been through a bunch but never this dramatic

With my pedigree, you'd think recovery was automatic

Tell y'all one thing all this pain and therapy y'all can have it

Can't give it away, so I guess I'll keep it

With adversities in place, my goals, will I reach it?

My foot, in its condition, don't feel like myself

Have to fight off plenty feelings of putting me on the shelf

The road has been hard and rough and still far to travel

I hope this experience doesn't make me unravel

If I do hope I can pick up the pieces

So I can continue to bring the universe, my rhyming thesis!!!

Confrontation

First time I faced racism, I was in the fourth grade

I couldn't believe the behavior this teacher displayed

I'm sure she couldn't believe what happened next

I stood tall, firm, erect shouted aloud demanding my respect

In front of the whole class, proceeded to show my ass

I labeled her a bigot, without thinking twice

The stare I displayed, colder than ice

She was shaking in her boots, nervous as ever

Did I give fuck? Nope but however

It had to be done, I'm really not the one

This act landed me in special education

All from performing verbal elation

You see respect works both ways

Not only now also in those days

Even then I knew racism wasn't right

That's why today, I continue the fight

I'll be damned if I let anyone, question my might!

I live with racism because I don't have a choice

What I won't do, is act like I don't have a voice

My words will be heard, whether they make sense or absurd

I've been given one life, so I'll live it as I please

So the bigots can miss me with the rhetoric & bullshit decrees

They claim to be superior but scientifically this is false

Without their power and money, that came from free labor, they would be lost

If the playing fields were leveled, we would see who would be boss

Coming or Going

I'm a Gemini, so I come divided

When answers are needed, which side will provide it?

Some not so good, others are the greatest

That's fine, catch a whiff of my latest

Inspiration, gotta practice more self dedication

True to myself, gotta know who I'm facing

It's me whom I'm referring to, isn't that amazing?

Constantly at battle with myself, a civil war of sorts

When I give myself trouble, I look to me for support

Funny thing is no matter the outcome, I'll always win

Whether I'm being an angel or indulging in sin

No matter the decision, I'm always right

With this battle going on, sometimes I don't sleep at night

It's a battle for the ages

All I can do is continue to turn the pages

On this book called life,

write new chapters

On a daily basis, embrace the pain and the laughter

I'll continue to write, seems to be great therapy

But the shy person in me, doesn't want the world staring at me

The outgoing part, has been itching to start, getting riches and accolades

That guy also would enjoy, bitches and escalades

The shy guy, can't even deal with the sun in his eyes

Let alone, book signings, allowing the world to spy

So this is with what I am faced

Do I send shy guy or the extroverted in his place?

Or do I send a mixture of the two?

Oh please help me self, what the fuck should I do??

Nothing and everything are the answers I receive

I go back and forth like you wouldn't believe

I guess a happy medium would be the answer

If it was that simple, I wouldn't sway back and forth like a drunken dancer!!

Blessed

Highly favored and originally flavored

I've been lost, and I'm still on the way back

This time, I'm surely on the right track

I've been this way since leaving the womb

God give the strength to make room

In my life, I'm close to my purpose

If I don't reach that pantheon, my life will have been worthless

Inspired to set the world a blaze

Not with fire but with vocabulary meant to amaze

Thoughts, Perceptions and Circumstances

Are About Ideas, outlook and second chances

Having thoughts, perception of what your plans is

The creator gave us a third eye to use

Take sometime out, give it a peruse

We've been taught we have 5 senses, in reality we have 6

This is just one of the devil's many tricks

With that in mind, it's so much more to discover

Instead of using the last five, use the other

I know u see last and it sparks confusion

Let me clear up this mass illusion

You see your third eye controls it all, in all it's splendor

Knowing this, for me anyway, impossible to surrender

My God given rights and such

Take a third eye trip, what are you willing to give, I pray not much!!!

After all what good is smell, taste, hearing, sight and touch

If your third eye, you are not in touch

Like the minimum wage, I promise, not much

Boasting

As I enter these lines on paper

Wheels going, thoughts brewing, there's my next caper

Funny how thoughts can materialize into material

Similar to when you get a hankering for your favorite cereal

First you check for milk, same as the sheet

Add it to cap'n crunch, corn flakes, same as when papyrus and ink meet

Vocabulary extensive, analogies by the dozens

That's why I know sheet, paper and papyrus can be considered cousins

Similes used, exhausted metaphors

Expand your mind and open doors

They help me get from one line to the next

Getting my thoughts off, similar to climaxing in sex

My foreplay with words is timeless

It's just a matter if time before I'll be considered one of the best

Verses come together, similar to bird constructing a nest

I'll tackle any topic, as if I was Ray Lewis

I know for sure I was put here to do this

I've tried several items and excelled at a few

Nothing as well as poetry, confidence soaring, it will leave me well to do

RockStar

I was lost and now I'm found

Pen to the paper, time to get down

Poetry flows, from my heart to the sheet

The more I write, the more I feel concrete

Solid as a rock, my words are bliss

One day soon, I'll be on the best sellers list

Attempting to put down language to which everyone can relate

I know I'm good, my ego, no need to inflate

Once my lyrics permeate the universe

All walks of life will relate to each and every verse

I can see clearly now, that the storm has passed

My literary skills, processed sand, you know glass

I brag and boast but my actions will speak the loudest

Gonna make my momma and my whole family the proudest

Words to the paper, like key to the lock

They come together like geese to a flock

AC/DC, Metallica, Led Zeplin yeah I ROCK!!

Mother's Model

Hey mom, just stopped by to chat

You ruined me, just want you to know that

I hold women to a standard, they can't seem to reach

Nowadays the values I saw my mom display, they don't seem to teach

I'm sick to my stomach, dealing with these half ladies

Quick to lie, cheat and be lazy, why are females so shady?

What happened to honesty, values and virtue?

This shit is beyond crazy, I just don't know what to do

It's not that I want to be with my mother

It's just I know what's possible and I don't enjoy the other

So thanks Ma, for my heightened standards, I won't settle for less

So for now I'll stay single and avoid the unnecessary stress

Maybe one day I'll find the one, until then I'm done with this relationship mess

I'm not claiming perfection, I have issues of my own

I do know the difference between claiming independence and really being grown

Ladies giving up the panties, doesn't make you an adult

Getting to know someone, inside and out, achieves this result

Girls get back to making men work for your treasure

Get to know if he's worthy of obtaining that pleasure

I'll let you in on a little secret

Respect and rapport is built, during the time that you keep it

So ladies take these words with a grain of sodium

And keep guys like myself, off the podium

I bring this advice, with love in my heart

Ladies respect yourself, from the end to the start

As a man we will be forced to play our part

My mother gave me counsel, that sticks with me to this day

She told me if she's quick to give it to you

Who else has she given it quick, to?

Don't get me wrong ladies, if your giving we're taking

If you do it too fast, more than likely, its a mistake that you're making !

Tales of the Hood

Botched Plan

I made moves to get back in the streets

At first it seemed to be a plan that couldn't be beat

Until everything that could go wrong did

I feel like I did when I was a kid

Frustrated, confused are just a couple of my emotions

Inside, a storm brewing, organized commotion

Gotta break even, can't take a loss

Recover my investment at any cost

Dabbling in the street, can make your judgement quite hazy

Gonna showcase my real talent, rhyming verses from A to Z

Working for myself has always been my dream

Gotta keep writing, head full of steam

Full steam ahead, keep the train on the tracks

Forget the idea of selling weed pills or cracks!!

Streets are watching

As the blade hits the plate

My mind enters into a different state

Concentration is essential

In order to reach your full potential

Coppers in abundance, fiends come in flocks

Bagging up all the shake and of course the rocks

The streets are watching, for this you can be sure

If your moves are sloppy, the streets you won't endure

They smile in your face, when you leave, they speak hate on your name

But being a hustler, is what they claim

But what they are is the total opposite

True hustlers don't have the time, to talk about others shit

The customers will try you every chance they get

Tell you they want a dime but eight is what you'll get

Last but not least, are the police, they are a beast

In conjunction with the snitches, they can bring you to you knees

Know one thing, they're playing for keeps

One false move, have you wearing stripes when you sleep

Just think, it all started from the blade hitting the plate

All the true hustler's, I know y'all can relate

This is a tale of how the streets can pull you in and never let go

Use it as a stepping stone and not a career decision

Trust your third eye, not your sight, you'll be surprised what you can envision

Any Day on the AVE.

I sit here, drinking on barley and hops

Watching the ave., on alert for cops

Transactions constantly transpire

Law enforcement consistanly conspires

To lock me away forever, gone never to return

I gotta stop doing this, when am I gone learn

I guess this week in cook county did a gang to convince

Had to get up and get out, you know, jump the fence

It's the lifestyle's fence I'm speaking of

Had to go, you know, show myself some love

Don't make an error, I'm a hustler and player always

I hustle on time clocks nowadays

And I play this game called life every now and again

I do both, elevated echelons, I'm winning now : and again!!

I'm sharing this tale from my tattered past

So when the time comes, you won't end up on your ass !

Hell or Highwater

Every time difficult times arise, to my surprise

While weathering the storm, I can still open my eyes

As long as I can open my lids, I can envision

How to keep my mind, body and soul out of prison

A tough act to follow, my life has been a rough pill to swallow

Adversities to the left, obstacles to the right

I know one thing, never gave up the good fight

Perseverance in abundance, tenacity should be my middle name

The life I was born to live, got to stand up and stake my claim

No minutes for excuses, no hours for despair

Throw down the first gauntlet, to success, a war I declare

I'm coming, running, guns out, barrels blazing

With similes, analogies, metaphors that sound quite amazing

Limitless potential, vocabulary display, showcasing my credentials

I've realized most of my issues caused by yours truly

Living through and realizing at the same time, couldn't be

more grueling

So to the trying times, I bid them farewell

Clear skies, sun shining, not a cloud in sight, as far as I can tell!!